Life in Poetic Pieces

Life in Poetic Pieces

Kristin Aardema Faigh

iUniverse®

LIFE IN POETIC PIECES

iUniverse books may be ordered through booksellers or by contacting:

iUniverse
1663 Liberty Drive
Bloomington, IN 47403
www.iuniverse.com
1-800-Authors (1-800-288-4677)

Because of the dynamic nature of the Internet, any web addresses or links contained in this book may have changed since publication and may no longer be valid. The views expressed in this work are solely those of the author and do not necessarily reflect the views of the publisher, and the publisher hereby disclaims any responsibility for them.

Any people depicted in stock imagery provided by Getty Images are models, and such images are being used for illustrative purposes only. Certain stock imagery © Getty Images.

ISBN: 978-1-5320-6618-4 (sc)
ISBN: 978-1-5320-6617-7 (e)

Library of Congress Control Number: 2019901033

Print information available on the last page.

iUniverse rev. date: 02/26/2019

Contents

To Janice F. Lewis, my amazing mother, for being constant

PART I

Nature

Gift

Poetry speaks
in so many tongues
of verbal nature, dramatization,
written word, daily life.
Poetry surrounds
all states of existence,
all forms of being,
brings life
to unborn concepts,
explains death into beauty.
Poetry lives
in all things—human,
animal, plant, inanimate,
spiritual …
Poetry's surface
remains smooth, still,
untouched.

Scroll

Knuckles whiten
from anxious pressure.
Pen stands tall,
anticipatory of motion.
Time becomes meaningless,
useless as thoughts flow
to pen point.
Hours pass from word
to word while new passages
are ventured in mind,
yet time has counted
only minutes …
Instrument is drawn
to sheet
as memory is no match
for written word;
explanation is fruitless
for vision best revealed
in poetic scroll.

Morning Forecast

Distant layers of color
softly uncover morning.
Sky is clear,
morning star bright;
half moon slowly dissipates
to light.
Warm air wisps
between cracks and gaps
of abandoned station.
Mildness of morning breeze
silently hums.
Cacti stand tall,
towering over the desolate sands
blowing timidly
about their trunks.
Ghost crab leaves its burrow,
skitters to another
several feet away,
shell reflecting iridescence
in this morning's glow.

Desert flora add hue
to prevalent blandness;
they wave slightly to and fro,
portraying life.
Mountains lie in shadow
as new light reaches
to their peaks.
Jagged tips pierce
the pastel sky
as morning sun bursts
into brilliance.

Vision

Watch the pond quiver
when a breeze skims its surface;
small bubbles appear from fish
searching for air.

Listen to quiet *tap-tapping*
as raindrops fall lightly on water;
rustling grows in an audience
of trees.

See waves lapping steadily
at a half-submerged dock;
tires sway to and fro.

Feel thunder rumble;
hear it roll across the sky.
A storm approaches
my mind's eye.

Of Trees

Tall, silent, powerful,
they stand,
beautiful or barren.
Years, decades, centuries, pass by,
their only statement a rustle
in seasonal breeze.

When frosted in white
they stand seemingly paralyzed,
brittle,
more silent still
than inanimateness.
Arms stretch skyward,
reaching for warm breath.

Birds sing an awakening;
closed fists burst open
into green canopy,
provide shade from hot sun.
Giants whisper softly;
raindrops rattle, pelt
their faces,
feeding deep veins.
They stand so vulnerable,
drinking of their own sweet breath.

As breeze cools, living giants become
vibrant with color,
speak loudly at last,
"Here I am. Behold my splendor!"

***

Then as quickly,
intense heat passes
in summer's wane;
bodice slowly crumbles.
Brittle, crackling fallen face
is swept away by new winds.
Season's fold
leads to slumber.

Lake at Night

Twinkling lights dot
and sparkle deep
in manganese blue
over water.
Moon smiles,
flowing white, grounded
in hue of night.
Starlight reaches down,
touching reflections
on softly rippling surface—
huge blackened pool
is alive with highlights
of sky and earthen
landscape.
Thin line of road
behind streetlamps
lies softly like yellow ribbon
draped as edging
to high hill above.

Slightly swaying trees
litter the top
as soldiers slowly descending
from battle, yet standing
forever tall in their pride.
Evening sounds whisper
moonlit secrets, grow in volume
as current shifts.
Tied boat at white dock tugs
eagerly at freedom,
seeking to drift away
in night's solitude,
find peace
from monotony of shore's lap.
Crowd of trees murmurs
well-kept secrets behind dock,
forever guarding
its captive scene.

Afternoon

I sit
in a field
of soft climbing blades
moving peacefully, endless
in sway.
An audience of pines
shields my back;
they whisper secrets
among themselves.
Far into blue ceiling
lies a dark line
of sweet-smelling giants,
reaching always to cover
evening's pastel glow.
Bright golden light dips westward,
holding back the coming of night.

I close my eyes
to absorb the cadence
of activity.
Breeze quietly whistles past,
tickling bare ears;
ponytail rubs shoulders
to cool with a tingle.
Slight shiver.
Below and around swarms busyness,
whirling into mind's array,
back to center, me, sitting
with pen growing hot,
paper waving
in unseen wisp.

Gulf Shore Walk

Sea salt rises
in aromatic swell.
Surf rolls, crashes,
crawling hiss on white beach
of crushed shell.
Black curtain lifts from horizon,
sliver orange moon peeks through
to lay shimmer on night sea.
We walk hand in hand,
breathe deeply of salty richness,
scan for treasures by sound
of clashing shell cases.
Giggles are silenced
in roar of powerful waves
while sidestepping,
reaching foaming arms;
embrace in deep shadow
of palm.

Dusk

Sparkles of light dance
about rippling water.
Scorching sand hisses
as breakers recede from shore.
Sparse strands of grass
lazily sway
in melancholy choir.

One seagull passes overhead;
its song follows it, then fades
into deepening sky.
Hollow log seems empty
yet is alive with ladybugs.

And an orange sun rests
on glowing horizon.
It slowly sinks
like a disk in oil,
then a brilliant green flash
swallows the scene.

Storm

Raging mountains roll
across brilliant slashing swords.
Drummer plays cadence.

Haiku

Betty M.

One loud person talks
too much in our group of mouths
speaking louder still.

Haiku

Leak in a Window Over the Writers

Sliver stream trickles silently
down brick wall
surrounding the writers
who read and chat.
It grows wider, cooler,
wetter—moistens our small room
at the library.
Voices begin to sound tunneled
around our circle of ever-spilling words,
close to walls bronzing
with crawling rainwater.
Hissing begins to roar
as writers' feet squelch
on soaking carpet,
tunneled voices rising
in volume to be heard
over rushing loudness.
Chairs become unsteady
as buoyancy climbs
above knees.
Windows fog with steamy bath,
roaring cave, floating table.
No concern until
everyone has a chance to read.

Pere Marquette

This day my spirit calls to feel the lake,
lighthouse staunch in ever-bullying current.
Fickle wind unseen but in the wave
of vessels bowing to court whitecaps' hiss.
Fishermen silently tend to pole and hook,
beckon unobtrusively in casting
lines to hungry seeking life, wait
patiently for them to make the choice.
Bollard of cold steel supports this soul
paradoxically warmed by sinking sun,
mind clearing of its incoherent rattle
through peaceful moments in the weather's thunderous silence.
Shadow leads to shore between jagged, cold rocks,
descending to shallower depths and a small commotion
of mallard drakes fighting quietly for a hen's favor.
She waits at hand to please the winning consort.

Day's Hike

Air grows thin with each step.
Exhilaration soars with adrenaline rush
while climbing dangerous rocky terrain,
exploring vast levels of mountain range.
Trees have long been left behind, their oxygen
only a dream now, yet it doesn't matter—
sky's blue surrounds me. Brightness warms
my back, even in the brisk of altitude. I
am free, burdened only by a backpack
filled with means of survival.
Releasing life's walls of business and obligation,
I experience life to the fullest, as it's meant to be.
I stop momentarily to look around,
become aware of conditions propitious to the climb,
and continue, undaunted by lack of air,
to reach the top, where I rest in awesome beauty.

Of This Autumn

Blue is laced with chill though sun still warms.
Leaves begin to burn with crimson tips,
golden like the glowing orb above,
reminiscent green of summer days.
Yet into this new season of hope and change,
insidious serpents have wound themselves like vines
around branches, trees thriving with breath
of life, only to squeeze it from some,
force labored breath from many touched
by the negative passage of time and loss.
Each day as autumn cools toward November's frost,
leaves begin to wither, float lifeless to earth.
As nature's imminent death falls on this land,
a stir can be felt, cogent thrust to face the truth
that remains unchangeable despite this fickle race—
choice exists to perish as leaves or vie for spring.

Lake Effect Blizzard in West Michigan

Wind hisses
in manganese haze
of blizzard. Houses
fade as night darkens.
Snow covers rooftops,
blows into piles
on doorsteps.
I await Husband's homecoming
in this hated weather,
probably more frightened than he
for his safe return.
Minutes tick by so slowly.
They feel like hours
as day disappears
in front of my bleary eyes.
House is empty,
loud in its quietness.
Thinking pounds
between ears, rumbling thoughts
tumbling into, over, new thoughts.
Fears in grasp of pessimism.
Watching night deepen to black,
I pray him home even
in whipping of white storm.

What is taking so long?
He should be home by now.
Phone doesn't ring—
I'm so alone.
What if he doesn't
come home? What then?
My best friend,
my love, I must
make plans … Consuming fear …
How will I tell the children?
Oh, don't leave me, man!
Fists hold head
in futile shaking
of this realization.
Telephone rings.
No! Don't answer. It
won't happen if you
don't answer!
Hand reaches.
Three rings, four …
"Hello?" I whisper,
tears already flowing freely
when I hear
the garage door open.

Elements

Sky is gray, earth is gray,
drizzle spatters, relentless,
upon growing puddles, hypnotic drone.
Traffic flows back and forth,
vehicles enter different parking lots
for similar reasons.
Red cars, green trucks, brown SUVs, yellow buses
deliver folks to work, take them home,
relentless in time, continuing
to march steady, steady,
caught in flowing system
of sameness, overwhelming body
of possibility passed by each day
on the way to work,
questioning where to turn,
where to stand,
where to be still.

Sky is gray, earth is gray,
drizzle spatters relentlessly
as my spirit strives for direction,
to find my place within God's plan
for this space and time that continues,
marches steady, steady, past
bright colors, evolving shapes,
laughter, sorrow, joy, grief.
Impatiently learning to wait in the midst
of this flowing river of sameness
and possibility,
beginning to realize
that January has changed.

Shape

Flame is constant light,
flickers, searching finger of heat
reaching into, creating, crevasse after crevasse,
tunnels of shadow, deeper moving,
shadow melting, molding—molten
liquid pools waiting for that final breeze, walls
ever changing, edges shining with liquid
erosion, expanding, constant shift in overall shape,
heat searching for an outlet,
contained, embalmed, deepening, rooting. Beautifully shaped
bubbles form, threaten to burst
but unable to—not quite enough substance or heat,
single flame not enough ... snuffed out,
light gone,
fragrance, spirit free, traveling upward ...
Pool cools, thickens, hardens. Liquid shine
disappears as warmth leaves. Waiting,
waiting for that certain spark to share.
Idea.

PART II

Life

Same Old Tune

Travel back in time
as notes tune, octaves ring out
in warmth and comfort of home.
Never is practice
so perfectly timed—
or anticipation of it—
as during the wait.
Mr. Whiskers and I sit curious
in a corner, being quiet
so as not to disturb.
Forever seems
an appropriate description
of the wait;
feeling a loss of precious moments
pulling at longing fingertips.
Suddenly fingers ache to play
Mozart, Grieg,
show tunes, Leroy Anderson.
Mind hears tunes all at once,
each being played,
blending into one song.

I pull close
my faithful dog, who looks at me
in puzzlement
when I begin to sway
to a secret melody.

Then trance is broken
as final notes sing,
octaves ring out,
sounding better as forever passes.
Still I travel back in time
to some decades ago—
same as now—
and wait
for the piano to be tuned.

Early Break

I miss my parents
and a youthful life,
all of us sitting together
at dinner.
We saw Europe in '74,
visited Florida every year.
Sure, brothers and I fought,
but a closeness was always there;
we were family.

I miss my parents,
not just for their loving hugs
but also for the security.
Things would be all right.
My home was just right—no place better
for living,
I thought.
During summer we water-skied, swam,
boated, canoed, had picnics,
enjoyed trips together.
I didn't know those times would ever end.
But they did.

At first I felt like a big shot;
nobody else's parents
were getting divorced.
(Alas, another time …)
Sometimes we were paid special attention to,

to ease the pain.
I thought I liked that, but secretly I wished
for my memories again to be real—
what was real now?
Were the memories ever real,
or were they just wishful dreams? It seemed
like so long ago I was that happy.

I learned to adapt;
we all seemed to—at least for a while.
My world no longer made sense
as I grew into a teen.
I grew angry
and desperate, feeling time was running out.
Everyone and everything seemed
to crowd in on me.
I had to get away—
and I did.
My reality had to be someplace else,
something I created—
and it was, but not how I expected.

Now I feel I need my parents more than ever;
I miss Mom and Dad together. My brothers are far away
with families, a life, of their own.
The happiest part of my childhood seems
so far away,
but I know it can't be recaptured;
that doesn't change my feelings.
I understand them; that's a start.

No one is to blame or should feel hurt
by these things. They lie on the page
as an aid to understanding
the way things are—

result of an early break.

Overwhelmed

Pool rises to my ankles,
slowly, unceasingly,
as I dig, dig deeper
into swollen cliff of clay,
remove piece after piece,
dropping them all into the pool.
And it rises.
My back grows sore, stiff,
weakened by digging motion.
Arms grow heavy as iron bars.
Countenance is grimace
beginning to melt
into rising eddy—
loss of distinction.

Fool

Mysterious is mind
when mind is without answer.
Mind's eye searches
through dark, endless corridors—
looking, looking …
There is ambiguity, doubt,
curiosity, concern,
frustration, sadness,
happiness, and maybe
love.

But knowledge is unattainable
when there has yet
been no thought.

Shame

Time spent, time wasted, times past.
Another time, because of time,
when it's time to …
Time forgotten, a remembered time,
time gone by.
Time slips, time cut short,
lack of time, when is the time,
now it's time,
yet
time's up.

To Solve

True realization of a concept
enhances thought.
Thought, as seed,
flourishes to further similar concepts,
which branch into ideas.
Ideas, when stimulated,
prepare objective conclusion formation.

Drawn conclusions, therefore,
focus
in on a distinct problem,
whereby an ideal search
begins.

Blind Ladder

Basic instincts of competition without understanding
focus on corporate battles
driven by educated brainwashing
that numbs the soul's hunger to later reflect
if one is lucky enough
to be able to touch the meaning of what
is really productive in a life.
What matters so much
that winning a way or a position to step
on the hem of others' journeys
in order to guide a dysfunctional goal
causes one
to reach up for a taste of respect?
All is a lie
in the universe of circular relationship
when fight has no effect upon the heart
and when derision rules strong through manifest courtship
as an encouraged malevolence plays its part.

Student of Life

Inspired by Philippians 4:13

This is a season of choices amid the wait,
Where opportunities present themselves as gates—
Not blatant but obtuse, to seem remote,
Calling for purposeful action in seeking the lot.
Unique paths, unclear in destination, beckon
To be explored with patience and in wisdom;
Their focus can be true or mired with temptation,
So discernment is needed through prayerful meditation.
What doors can be opened are yet unknown to me—
The ways of God's plans I have not foreseen,
Except to realize, indeed, there is a plan;
Therefore, I must risk to take a stand!
Possibility exists within the guise of the world.
As Christ reveals through my search, this becomes unfurled—
In the meantime I'll be as I'm called to live today,
Remembering all things are possible when done God's way.

Hope

The difference between autonomy and desperation
is a line that seems so thin
yet worlds apart, pulled taut by ropes,
binding thought from breath, revelation from pulse.
Youth is drained from time held captive
within four walls of seeping deceit
so subtle to cause blindness of spirit
that cries out nonetheless
for truth, happiness, a door to bud
from solid obstacle, awaiting discovery
of light, joy, peace, breath caught
in gasp of fresh air, sweetened
by the touch of grace.
When it comes, is coming, brilliance
shines in smiles, stolen glances,
peace in silence between conversation.

Education

I thought I was right.
He thought I was wrong.
His having an "upper hand"
in the matter
made me wrong.
There was no recorder
in the room taking notes.
So no record verbatim
of what was said
exists.
I heard what he said,
though he disagrees,
because he said something other
than what I heard.
Was there lack of communication
on his part?
Or lack of understanding
on mine?
Who is responsible for misinterpretation
of a concept?

Discovering Self

Find a place,
young imposter.
Find a place
in which to stand, on which to build;
plant trees and flowers,
perennials.
Fashion a nest out of particles
from here and there;
call it home.
Watch others, listen closely,
embrace opportunity.
Stand solid in quicksand,
for there is purpose in all being.

Search on for knowledge;
do not look for answers
but create them.
Look ahead with guidance
and spirit.

Challenge awaits a hungry heart.
Experience life; make possible
discovery of self.

Flesh

Passion, opinion, pride, worldview, judgment—
all are emotive burnings in the flesh.
Variety and scope surface unexpectedly
in face of sudden shifts in the air
that can go almost unnoticed by a stranger,
perplexing to an innocent heart, at fault.
Hypocrisy is a strong word to use
when one is so enrapt with specific focus,
absorbed in valued images and meanings
that have shaped life to where one is at present.
But whether or not this word sounds harsh, it fits
into place when shoes are walked in by another.
A whole new world can be seen through different eyes,
humbly touched in seeking another's truth.
It goes both ways when looking at offense,
where also lies the lack of intended mock.

Achieving Success

Everything I need is already present
In my heart, only waiting to be discovered.
All it will take is overcoming the obstacle
Of perceiving myself unworthy of achieving success.
I know my true home is not of this world
In which I must fight to be who I am
Amid the strong temptation to conform
To mundane goals and twenty-first-century culture dictates!
Keys to unlocking the dream rest in two Trinities,
First in Creator, Christ, and Comforter.
In accordance with the very highest power
Is body, mind, and spirit, soul's trinity.
I will seek and find these keys through my heart's assent,
Be patient in the process, stay open to wisdom
Of persons who have succeeded, learning still
To follow the Source of life with adamant joy!

Modernity

Laboratory mice
in a maze
running,
looking for food,
seemingly content in their state
of imprisonment.

They haven't noticed
a little hole
on the same path run,
a little hole
in need
of a little encouragement
to grow
into a doorway.

Post Modernity

Laboratory mice
in a maze
running,
looking for more,
no longer content in their state
of imprisonment.

They have noticed
a little hole
on the same path run,
a little hole
they are turning into a doorway
with a little encouragement.

Jury Duty

I sit alone
among twelve others,
all of them alone as I.
We sit as judges
in a box, set above
others present.
I look straight into
the eyes of a man
bound
for trial, believed
guilty but held
innocent until guilt
is proved.
I sit in my chair,
guilty myself of lesser
crimes punishable only
by self, yet placed here,
today, to judge a man
I know nothing about
by word of mouth
and shuffles of paper.
He speaks not for himself
but allows another speak
for him, a paid
defender of justice,
though his own beliefs
may differ in words

fallen from tongue.
Emotions thrust thoughts
into this naive mind. *Guilty,
guilty, guilty,* runs over
and over like record,
though I know nothing
of this man except that
he waits
as defendant, pleading
not guilty to a charge not
easily put upon an innocent man.
Who am I to judge him? I ask
myself continuously, quietly
in the back of my mind.
His Honor sits only
as referee, for we are
omnipotent on this day.
He listens, as do we, to four
different testimonies
of the same words.
I find my emotions quelled
as the trial continues, changed
from verdict reached through ignorance
to unavoidable verdict reached
through evidence.
I try hard to find
the man's innocence—
could this be the wrong man
falsely accused of this
terrible deed, wrong place,
wrong time? I find
there is no alternative
to my judgment. I must trust
words from the law, persons
though I know them not,
but there is oath involved here,

personal promise to uphold
the rights of others, and
this man who will be
punished appropriately
for his wrongdoing.
Will it change him?
Thirteenth juror discharged.
With thanks, it is time
to deliberate, though we
have done this individually
already—it is time
to make the final decision,
change the man's life for good
or not for good,
his choice in the first place;
this will not take long.
As we file back
into our seats, final
deliberations over, thundering
silence falls upon this
dark courtroom. I no longer feel
a part of the scene, but rather
a spectator viewing the performance,
awed by the reality of show.
Then I feel my lips part, voice
speaking the words thought
originally in so different a context:
"Guilty, guilty, guilty."

Quiet Playhouse

In the center of town
sits a quiet playhouse
closed tight,
many years abandoned.
Its walls are bright blue—
lettering, thespian faces shining
white in sunlight.
Doors are boarded shut.

Inside crowds dazzled
to poetic intrigue, sonnets
sung in tears, mysteries
solved through long moments
of tension, beauty in musical storytelling.
Lives changed in affect
from emotion backstage,
onstage, behind curtain
left, curtain right.
Painted faces hid past,
present, possibly portraying
future, colorful mask.

Audiences swarmed in seats
to get a laugh, a cry, get away—
casts emulating stardom
to create laughter, tears,
impressions, remembrance.

Together they climaxed then parted,
each separated by personal
drama, yet forever joined
by the experience.

Now hallway sits
in darkness, theater empty
of any heartbeat; there is
no mention backstage
in the throes of curtain call
preparation. Yet inaudible rumble
grows within these walls
joined secure, growing year
after year, searching
for an outlet
to explode.

Immanent Presence

Fear
Exists
At the tip
Of ideas,
Which are different
From illusions
Of the safe
Borders
Known.

Fear Surfeit

What's really under the bed
or hiding in the darkness
of a closet?
What fiendish being lurks
in simple hometowns?
Who or what plagues
the homes, nightmares,
or memories
of the mundane human
being?

Monsters of subconscious
are kept in check,
though sometimes
weakness calls forth their power,
and they reign for however long
it takes.

From space, blackness, hell,
they come,
hiding in corners
of eyes; they are shadow
yet substance—reaching
with outstretched hands.

What now grasps
life's pleasures—
causing fear—
finds shelter in Richard Bachman's
alter ego.
His spry imagination
breathes.

Magnificent Fear

For David Leestma

Close my eyes
in a dream
of starry night.
Lift high my vision
to heaven, behold
this longing
to be part
of my universe.
Hold my breath
in blastoff
as seconds seem hours
in uncertainty.
Let me breathe
deeply, slowly,
as Earth is left behind;
I am space bound!
Feel pounding, thunderous silence.
Movement almost impossible
as seconds last days.

Let me know
the tingling excitement
waiting to explode
in bursting energy—
magnificent fear that churns
insistently within my soul.
Let me be
joyous!
Open my eyes
to see
the starry night. Fly
high to become one
with my universe!

Flight of the *Atlantis*, 1992

Monologue #1: Thoughts concerning Business, My Role in Its World

In less than a century, industrial's age
put the world into vacant frenzy
of fast-moving days, and along the way it
left behind many who feel lost,
in need of touching inherited pasts!
I am not machine; I am a human
being—no wonder I search anachronisms
for the meaning of who I am,
where I belong, where I came from.
But I am guided toward God's purpose,
distracted from wiles of this world's scene,
though swept along quicker than
I can reverse its conveyor,
twentieth century having picked me up
and driven straight into its system.

Life was good for me in childhood,
when imagination was encouraged,
wood free to roam. There was time.
A score and some are gone, and were considered waste,
yet not more than vision's preparation,

a shaping through currents of pain and confusion,
awaiting conformity. It almost occurred
as survival's struggle continued to press
on, compelling desire to wage
war against status quo—the easy way
for some, right way for others, loss for many.
What now? Surge ahead into a life of business,
being recruited like an animal baited to trap,
selected not for who and whose I am,
but for skills achieved through struggle,
again for survival, not where the heart leads.
No! This is temporary as I grow
into who and whose I am, God's child,
not to walk in ways of this world I see,
but to stretch myself accordingly to be
one of many who do not belong
in this realm of speed and ease of thought,
the swiftness that takes away song
sung in happy labor created
by hands and heart in love and praise to God,
though anything worthy can be done in praise to God!

Coming down hard on "human resource management,"
I freely admit I am, and I agree
with Paulo Freire: "The answer lies
not in the rejection of the machine, but rather
in the humanization of man."[1]

This is my purpose: not
to bring profit to corporation,
but to love others as I am loved
by God, who teaches me

---

[1] Paulo Freire, "Educating for Critical Consciousness." Sent with a letter to Pope John Paul II, who responded through Monsignor Pedro Lo'pez Quintana, Assessor.

to write, to act, to sing, to listen—
to be true to the gift,
(to rebuke vanity accompanying it),
and to perform readily
as a joyful slave of Christ.

PART III

Family

Tough Love

The time between beginning and the end
is oft forgot because it is so hard,
when scourge of heart, the battle fought within,
slowly destroys this organ once so ardent.
Gravity takes its toll on smiling lips
as strength is wan in sorrow, expression forced.
Why now this body fails beneath the tumult,
as crowded years of chaos have been common?
Why now, as joy has touched this aching soul,
love blooming for the first time and allowed
to rest on wisps of hope beneath the sheltered
layer upon layers of survival skills
verily often needed from day to day?
Truth be told, prayer's answers are forthcoming—
arduous task at hand and heart apparent
in humanity's continuous struggle with laws of nature.

Little Girl

Bright glow up and to my left,
shines, streaks
upon my doll.
Her smile stretches to half moon.
Big round eyes sparkle green,
filled with love.
Her arms flop heavy
up and down as I drag
her stuffed body, almost as big
as mine.
She wears ribbons
and has hair to comb,
button nose, freckles everywhere.
She is my favorite,
only one with pocket and hanky;
I love her, and she hugs me back,
pushes and kicks me.
Tie her shoe, buckle
other, make a bow
trailing gently down red locks
hidden under green linen scarf.
I will tie her shoe, buckle it
again, again, sit
under the bright, hot glow
till I can tie my own.

Grano

Forty years ago, more and less,
you listened to silly stories
of animation, seen through the eyes
of your granddaughter;
she could tell stories too.
You listened with such interest;
your attention never left
the child—hasn't still.
You washed dishes
together—
granddaughter stood tiptoe
on two-step ladder, her favorite
because it was yours.
She could still smell Sunday dinner
as dishes were slowly wiped,
faint aroma of those magical chocolate chip
cookies of unequaled recipe,
hot sweetness of blueberry pie,
even when none was served
with dinner.
Your patience
made an afternoon last
as grandchildren waited for storytelling,
time to gather around
dark green rocking chair that lives
still in heart,
each begging for a favorite story,

never disappointed
as each wish was granted.
Your house was never crowded,
never empty, as its walls absorbed
your magic and hold it still
wherever you file cabinet sits—
cozy, simple, with love
and grace.

Dear GraMpa

Mailbox stands waiting
where lie my grandfathers,
their bodies at peace
in bone and ash, trees
flourishing remembrance
of busy lives too short
for my liking.
They went away
when I was nine,
passing on to their
next journey
so gracefully,
sadly to Grano and Nanny,
Mom, Dad,
and us, their grandchildren,
though our understanding was limited.
Now the years roll by
through new lifetimes,
traditions, experience,
as memory of their ultimate transition
remains in the mind of a
nine-year-old child.

Though years and years
have flown thus and continue
to pass like wisps of air,
my memories of them thrive
as they thrived for sixty-six, sixty-five years,
and I wish to know them
better. I think
I'll write a letter.

Companion

You who lie
on quilted spread
with supple ears, stubby tail,
soft, silken belly.
You who gaze in earnest
with big brown eyes,
lashes a half foot long,
wanting to satisfy my every whim.
Only a dog.
You who walk steadfast
at my side,
through anger, love, and pain,
know my thoughts
at sidelong glance.
Only a dog.
You who act as child,
annoying so briefly,
loved so dearly as
extension of myself.
Only a dog, you
are my closest companion.

Miracle!

Someone within has changed
this, myself.
At once I am shared
with another!
Unknown dark vision grows
as part of me, flesh
within flesh,
soul within soul.
Speak to me,
little one who touches
my heart.
Tell me
of this someone
who hungers to see light!

Child's Touch

Hold my hand, little one;
don't let go!
Walk with me
through passageways.
Tell me to slow down
if I run,
to walk faster
if I drag my heels.
Help me to see a simple solution
to adult complexities.

Follow close, little one;
travel with me
as I walk long beaches,
listen to roaring waves crash
on shore, then hiss
as they recede.
Skip lightly with me
on a field.
Let us pause
to smell daffodils and lilies.

Pass through crispy brown woodlands
at my side,
then lead me onward
to the brilliant glow
of starry night,
to tomorrow.
Stay with me, little one.
Keep me young forever.

At the Beach

Climb, baby, climb
up the dune to its top;
green blades will bow
for your passage.
This is your ultimate freedom,
king of sandy mountaintop,
blissful in your pink nakedness.
Sparks of light dance
in happy blue eyes
as you stand with arms raised high
in triumphant stretch.
Teeth shimmer in wide grin
as dusk sun sets its rosy hue
upon your tiny chest.
Stand still now, baby;
don't move at all
while I set the lens
to telephoto.

Evolution

I have stepped this surface
hundreds, perhaps more, times.
Gray, chill afternoon, spring
trying bulbs to color.
Street noise, people—
shuffling of everyday surround.
Then a pause, not in stride,
but mental blink
to forever past.

I am
moving double time for a single
stride in this very place.
I am
one and small
beneath vastness of crisp blue,
walking clumsily
in a larger shadow cast on concrete.
Young and happy, my dreams
of future enhance reality,
which is
the whole experience
of childhood.
I clutch softness,
warmth of my future's guide.
My eyes are clear,
not yet clouded

by knowledge and experience gained
in growth, when reality
fades sometimes
to memories of carefree days
that were long,
and future seems
an untouchable thing. Time
stands still
more than once
as life's stages pass.

Smile creased lips then
and does now in bustling lot;
grayness seeps
back into vision as breeze
stings my cheeks. So
much is different—I am
mother, learned
of necessary things
only imagined, forever past.
Life's stage is shortened
as time flashes by eyes
clouded with focus and limitation.
I cast the shadow
tagging along in my secure grip,
whose future I struggle
to guide.

First published in "Poet to Poet" section of the *Writer*, March 1992.

How Was School Today?

On my way to school
I saw three dinosaurs.
They made me late
because they wouldn't move
until I said the Pledge of Allegiance.
My teacher was sick today,
so a very smart orangutan
read us stories all day
in US History,
about giants and sea serpents
and flying saucers.
At recess I noticed the sand
had turned purple, and the playground
equipment was chasing
Mrs. Johnson's fifth-grade class.
For lunch we enjoyed live beetles
with cranberry sauce.
I'm sorry I was late getting home,
but a frightened giraffe
asked how to get to the police station
(her purse had been stolen),
so I gave her directions.
An average day.

My Other Children

I needn't ask
my friends
to sit close; they
need no invitation.
Silky furs drape themselves
over my calves;
I am warmed
by purring cuddles
emitted so effortlessly,
generously,
from their little bodies.
My lap holds also,
upon any sitting that occupies my day,
black softness, bearded white,
brown eyes, snoring noisily,
tuned in only to my movements, desires.
When I must move, they follow,
never leaving me alone
for long.
My morning alarms,
evening's TV companions,
never getting enough sleep
but when on me.
Blessed animals, they are
my other children
of years longer than
human mothering.

Little girls lick quietly
their calico, tabby coats,
eyes thin slices in contentment
of massage.
Little boy—big
I should say—wagging stump
in such childish, loving way,
wash my hands clean
that I may stroke your satin ears.
Caring friends, I thank you
for filling these times
with such warmth
and acceptance.

Detour

Brittle leaves crackle,
roll across the avenue.
Wind hisses north and south
in sudden gusts;
sky lowers a heavy gray tarp
over everything.

Radio hums quiet company
in the little car,
while baby plays with a new toy;
traffic is sparse,
providing opportunity
for sideward glances
at poor homeless citizens
wrapped in skimpy blankets,
pulling along small crying shadows.

Baby smiles blue twinkles,
happy, carefree, innocent;
the heart is stabbed
with sudden compassion.
Yellow light, swaying
in gust of dead leaves,
blinks cautious passage
through the intersection.
Driving is slow in this

inner-city bleakness.
Foot lays heavy on accelerator—
four doors lock one world in,
one world out.

Visit

Father
fishes with his
grandson at Pere Marquette.
Though pain is screaming within his hip,
he gives.

Long Distance

I run
to the telephone
when it rings, hoping
a caller wants me.
Though salespersons are low
on my preference list,
the chance to have a
conversation
with an adult
excites me.

Children are great; I
love mine,
yet there is need
for stimulation other
than a frightful decision
between yogurt and a jelly sandwich.

Then there are times
like now
when I find it difficult
even to touch
the quiet, waiting telephone.

Dial tone sounds so lonely,
distant, droning on, on, till
touch tone beeps
from my fingers' memory.

This number is painful too,
of late,
never feeling right,
like past years when
often dialed two, three times daily.
Am I now the salesperson,
caller to an uninterested party
whose conversation
will be a silent no
to my one-sided dialogue?

The Yearly World

For Jeannie

I visit it
once a year,
the silent world
of Mary and Hannah,
where a loom rests
in use-worn body
atop fifteen darkened, winding steps.
Dimly lit hallway narrows
to bed and bath, unused.
This is Mary's floor alone
to live, to weave,
to live in perpetual silence.
She sits on stout bottom
as part of her daily craft,
aged so far into age unspoken,
not even watching the years pass.
She spins and weaves
with ardent satisfaction
of a nine-
or ten-dollar sale, perhaps,
keeping one eye on top step,
where her loathsome sister
may not tread.

And Hannah does not break
this unheard, unspoken rule.
But her lean, crumbling figure sits
with me at the kitchen table,
speaking incessant gibberish,
language unknown to me,
though we understand each other.
Hannah is always excited
to have this company,
eager to offer her meager resources,
quick to accept warmth
of a handshake or hug
from this yearly visitor.
And on she talks
in squeaks, hoots,
and yowls of nonsense
to my smiling face,
while she boils a hot dog
or butters a slice of bread.
She shows me the newest thing
in her life, then things
I've seen before, interjecting
now and then a
reference to her wretched
younger sister.

I visit it
once a year,
the quiet world
of survival, companionship,
and curious hostility between
these two ancient women.
I am saddened
by their circumstances.
I cannot involve myself more
lest guilt of their burden fall

upon my shoulders.
One day, one hour,
can I give
to this lonely world,
though it is here always
in my heart.

Bipolar Sea

What is it like to live in the sea
With looks of a human, though countenance dark?
How does it feel to live alone in the sea,
Pretending to be part of the school
That carries the age of this generation?
How do you justify slipping through reeds,
To dip and feed in a strike,
When the school above willingly seeks
To surround you in nurturing love?
What will it take to make you look up
From the silt that draws you to graze,
To dig for pearls where oysters don't bed,
Crawl on limbs unsuitable for your kind?
Why persist in stealing others' breath
When you have so much available freely?
How will it be when hooked and drawn nigh,
Being too late for one more offered chance?

Awakening

What might it take for us to say
Words spoken by us every day
Simply, as you and I would greet hello?
Why must it be torturous to know,
Or hear, or see, or feel natural things
Such as this—I am awed to bring
Back, or do I feel for the first time,
Wholeness longed for ever behind
Shadows of a painful past still
Lurking in brightness of my heart?
The swooning state has already fallen
Around trembling voice, heart willing
To trust—myself, first of all—and
Face inevitability of rejection again (yours or mine),
Though right now I smile and enjoy this gift
Without expectation or promise from a kiss.

Second Chance

I weep, and Spirit speaks deeply through my tears,
Comforting visuals spoken by prophets in mind.
Yet a bilious circle of query dances in fear
Of repeating past chaos already lived.
I struggle to rediscover settling of mind
As mind seems to require shutting down.
My understanding seemingly fails to find
Logic through agenda in the round.
I rejoice in knowing the past will die away,
Though laying to rest the process causes me pain.
Although looking within new focus every day
Is a courageous journey, with you, I choose to take.
I am energized now with Spirit's redirection
Of my heart that was chained to another's damaged ideal.
You and I look forward together with curious predilection
As we live our dream's possibility as it becomes real.

Plain Brown Eyes

Colors, places, feelings, shapes, and images.
Rolling wisps of energy making up each day's
Essence—quiet hope present in analogous
Mind looking at green, at brown, to stay
Focused on life. There was time to dream when young,
Seeing grand ideals completed and in our grasp,
When possibility and reality seemed a natural progression
Of step by step, oblivious to probable lapse
Within the instability of a world separate from truth's dimension,
Endlessly rolling toward perpetual turmoil
Among the vacillating hearts of human beings.
Yet within the staging of this tragic guile,
Light, home, hope, definition, and ideal
Beat stronger than the curse of human nature—
A love surpassing possibility, becoming real
In plain brown eyes, my vision now, promised future.

Leap of Faith

This bird can't wait much longer to fly,
Wings feeling strong in urgency
To breach the barriers that keep earth from sky,
Oppress in fear's embrace so willingly,
Made to look as though it is the way—
For some, alas, but holding others back
From soaring above limits to human eyes,
Awakened by a chance to rise from lack
And see magnificence in this life where there suffers
Ageless cries out of misunderstanding
Heard endlessly through weeping hearts of fathers
Who yearn to make all right in babies' longing.
This bird stretches her wings in preparation
For flight from this deeply buried stolon
To be a light birthed from new creation,
Cradled in trust that flight is not alone.

PART IV

Spirit

A New Song

My soul seeks
the open door close by,
palpable.
I hear wind blow
through leaves, exposing their underbellies,
expecting rain.

I write these words
in objective surroundings,
daily obligation,
while unseen arms stretch
and pull my heart to be lifted
by the breeze.

Time passes, unstoppable in regret.
Sun rises,
falls, despite the rush.
I strive just to be, not think anymore
of what was or was not;
the rain has come and comes again.

I am lifted now
by unseen arms
to be the wind in my face,
follow a new song beckoning,
relentless,
toward all things.

Lyrics #1, Philippians 4:13

Church

Actively waiting to see where we will go,
Facing limits only by our human thoughts
Tossing to and fro as in a wind
That blows vessels bound from shore to shore
In sight of mortal eyes, yet blinding some.
But when to the self we seem to die,
Release the sail, and listen newly well,
The still, small voice grows strong to tell
Of where to go and guides in what to do;
To live lives fulfilled, we must follow through,
Ride valiantly through forests sight unseen.
Shielded by faith in our highest visioning,
Who steers vessels to soar unimaginable realms,
Meets the heart's desires in midflight,
Achieving blessing in life's most ultimate sight
Now, the present, as Creator's vision unfolds!

Walking

I know where I am headed down this path,
Walking
At a pace comparable to wheels,
     Walking
To clear my mind, too fast to ponder,
        Walking
To exercise tight knots in flesh, I wonder,
         Walking
About waves crashing salt on sand,
          Walking,
Shells grating beneath my feet, blistering.
           Walking
Waking senses dulled by obligation, hearing.
         Walking.
Herons' whispers fly, palm to palm,
        Walking,
Following close to watch my progress from
     Walking
Here to there and back, rest in the waves,
   Walking,

Shallows caressing neck, back, hips,
Walking
Before the winds awake, cradled in gentle surf,
    Walking,
Head held by God above, drowning tide,
       Walking,
Renewed to climb the stilts where I abide,
        Walking
Till again my heart is called to greet the shore,
        Walking.
My mind can touch serenity's hand once more.
        Walking.

Beyond the Dissident Dance

Embraced by God, who
is neither male nor female
but Spirit and Fluidity,
I am free
to move beyond oppressive culture
of patriarchal society, to move
into fiber of my being,
being spirit
formed with purpose, intent, and beauty,
not to declare my independence
of humanity,
yet to embrace again the spirit
of human being,
neither male nor female,
yet fluid and chosen and beloved,
free to choose my way
according to whose I am,
created to touch a few, or many,
who are open to Creator's purpose
in and through me
within the fallibility of this life adventure,
to live quietly awakened and always discovered
even within a shell of imperfection,
which is righteous in Christ's perfection.

Continue to use my voice to exhort
and empower, continue to use my arms
to embrace and console, continue
to use my legs to journey and dance,
continue to place on my heart God's Word
for me and yield
to its breaking with anticipation.
I am gentle bearer
of the Sacred Feminine, beloved
feminine of Universal Spirit,
filled with wisdom surpassing ages, waiting
only to be discovered and shared.
I am carrier of life's essence through knowledge,
life experience, capacity to nurture,
and I am celebrated within perfect Soul's loving embrace.

Lament

Oh, my God, why
do You not open the eyes
and hearts of Your people
to see and be set free from this torment
that rages even unbeknown to their souls?
We are clueless, Creator God, of the beauty
that is within Your heart—
You draw us ever nigh
with the love of Your Son Jesus,
yet we do not come nigh.
We hate, we kill, we manipulate,
we lie, we steal, we beat our
own breasts
with unmerciful weaponry,
destructive comfort, impertinence
for the very Spirit that gives us life.
Lord, my soul aches for glimpses
of Your glory that have touched
my heart of hearts.
But this fallible gentle cannot
make them see.
You must, O my God!

But yet I rejoice, my Creator God,
for Your mercy shown unto me and many
who rest in our brokenness of spirit and body,
made available for Your pleasure and content.
Oh thank You, Parent God,
for the inheritance that is mine, to be
Your beloved daughter, to see,
through these fallible lenses,
proof of Your love through Jesus the Christ,
Your very own Son and Self, who sacrificed Himself
just for me.
I rest, almighty God, patient
in Your patience
and full of hope for this humanity
that cannot transcend itself,
but which You, oh triune God,
transcend to and take us, beaten and cursed,
unto Yourself.

Seeing Her Emerge

For Marcia

Amazing to witness healing
as Jesus changes perception
of worldly chaos and harm.
Even infant fear and neglect
are transformed into peace and love,
experienced within Spirit's presence.

Healing is complete in Christ already,
but broken gestalts exist
in seen world, sensed until
released in love, which is the only perception
of which we were formerly capable.
Radiant energy (quantum physics)—the mind sees
so much more and yet
does not see the possibility beyond
what exists in experiential perception.

What is yet unknown, unknowable,
becomes emergent in some
as desperate hope in unwept tears
pushes to the surface.

And I am blessed witness, guide
within God's work, witness
to layered emotional brokenness falling away
and revealing the healthy core,
brass rings of strength
that had remained just out of reach,
though they had belonged to her
all the time.

To Ponder

What if we creatures,
when we return to Creator,
when we escape limitations of flesh
and modesty of mind, lose scales
from eyes,
become one with eternity.
Become?
Will bliss forget history, experience,
love, in Perfect Love?
Or will it not matter
As Oneness knows all
before time began?
Is benevolent madness
in gentle orbit of humanity
a tasting of bliss—
or just violation in time continuum?

In this history of independent poverty,
blow follows blow
as self-sufficiency and
ethereal "communication" numb
our humanity in sophisticated drudgery.
Instant, blatant, merciless consumption
dulls senses, self-awareness,
free will transformed into willfulness,
subjugated familiarity.
Incessant popping

of thoughts before they are thought,
living with malaise of warring insanity,
environmental demise,
hands financially tied tight
from desire to act, being drawn
to book, to know, to be known
by others, safely, longing for tenderness,
stimulation,
blood—
life force experienced by some
only through violent hatred.
Numbness becomes sought
as there is no more time to dream,
to be still and know
within this history's chaos,
which is no different
than past history except
in appearance.

Ultimate Reality beckons trust,
in obedience,
to embrace poverty
as others embrace its consequences
through just providence.
The Word brings back focus, but
the more studied,
the more learned, the more confused,
the more certain
of how little known—
yet creature feelings grow on in fog,
and clarity—
peace touched in soft, warm fur, panting smile,
quiet wisdom and playfulness amid spinning
of one sort or another, seemingly endless.
Is seeking goal
for something beyond ourselves

this comfort,
staid in unanswerable question,
and, perhaps, can pain be forgotten,
theoretically,
and bliss apprehended in ecumenical temple?

PART V

Death

Plague

Uncertainty looms in the face of chaos
As one mishap, illness, follows another.
Life seems a series of endless mountain climbs,
A slow-moving wave filled with screaming voices
Crying to get out and stop the madness,
This constant pain of insecurity.
Is there a way to quell the licking flames
That feast on, tease, consume aching flesh,
Or must endurance be the battle waged?
Can harmony lift up to sing above the mire?
Can joy be reinforced through constant praise?
When will this cease to be formidable battle
Of unwelcome surprise at every turn?
Did something happen to throw life out of line,
A step, perhaps, out of conventional status quo
Toward realms beyond where humans are bidden to go?

Pride

It is said that "pride goes before a fall."
What about when pride comes
after a fall—when party who claims hurt
is not the only party hurt?
Source has passed on,
no longer a being garnering need,
using voice, yet some are unsure
of where they stand.
Yes, I was born third,
but the fourth came sixteen years later
and, without biology,
reaped the good years
without baggage oppressing emotion.
Joy in like mind, they,
pain in the past for me mixed
with times of bliss—attention, approval.
Yet no anger is harbored,
only sadness, and separation—
void laid to rest
through gentle release of grasp.

Tyranny of Ego

Emotion has color—
sometimes sick yellow dripping
with death's stench, unresolved,
at times gray, cold, dark, drear,
hanging heavy in delusion of right,
not of Christ but so powerful—
red-brown brick with sides, angles, sharpness,
drawing blood, stacked one
upon another, held weak by drooping shoulders,
knees weakening under strain of lift,
juggling wall crushing breath
and life, other cheek failing to turn,
obliterated under load.
Sides cannot be chosen
in crumbled wall surrounds.

Everything has changed; nothing remains
familiar. Very quiet in this heavy tallow,
crumbled wall of shame covering
wretched, vomited ego.
Pain remains heavy like putrid crushed bricks
still commanding silent ache.
All must be rearranged, changed, rehued,
renewed for any dim light's penetration.
Seek growth in strong hue of hope,
strength regained like green grass growing,
translucent, full of glowing radiance

through seemingly endless weight
of drear and dread and hopelessness
to bursting bright sunshine in love's
Source, unseen for so long under
weighted load of thick layers,
not needing any longer to be held
by fingers dripping delusion's blood.
Retribution must not be resisted but embraced.
Evil's sting is lifted when patient endurance
shines, ruling the day—structure of pain falls
into black void, unable to regroup
in fallacy of fear: a new year.

Edge of Soul

Images flash and swirl
near edge of soul,
blend and vibrate as color
just out of cognitive reach.
Memories juxtapose with pain,
joy, hope, despair, reaching still
toward conscious discernment,
yet kept just beyond
mental grasp;
for whose sake?

Sibling biology so very close,
emotions roiling in father's loss.
What may be allowed to return
to mind, to be remembered
in honor of life lived,
children loved by perceived condition,
Mama's pain more evident in divorce
of covenant, made so young
at such a different time.

The ideal was there
in career, freedom of shelter,
food, European exploration in '74.
Family fun, Mona Lake, tennis,
Florida, Montana,
California after the falling apart,

struggle for sanity
in the midst of Hope College, bloody knees,
weekly visits, and escargot.

This is life, each day struggling
to meet ideal, failing daily
through double vision, which turned
ideal upside down. Still looking
to possess images near edge of soul,
watch them dart in between and around
waves of courage and fear—choices
and options not always well met,
yet justified often with food or drink.

Death's offerings of grief and pain
differ according to what one will allow
and strength of effort to hold back—
the pain swirling near the edge
if it has not been approached
for a time,
lingering quietly near edge of soul,
nay, screaming for full attention
to be viewed and laid to rest
with the deceased. An empty layer
filled with light of peace
rather than of void, yet filled with tears.

There is no preparation
for deep grief, though some grief
can be processed while life still holds.
No one expects hidden things
near edge of soul
to be exposed.—
what one wishes to embrace sorrow
in this day of reason?

Avoidance only works
for so long. Feelings must be felt—
life requires this, yet alone
feelings can overwhelm and overcome.
How can siblings so separated
by loss, anger, fear, lack of understanding,
find each other again?
Not by confrontation,
yet perhaps through time
and gracious encounters
at edge of soul.

Funeral

New era darkens
as night falls.
Dingy gray turns
to starless ebony.
Shadows appear
from nowhere;
they loom and grow,
black as night,
into fearsome bearers
of death.
Souls roam the streets,
bent, tired, looking
for pathways back
to a time before age.
One by one
they fall
into the darkness
covered by shadows
of time
moving on.
Aura of this town
grows fetid
as decay consumes
crumbling boundaries;
ashes to ashes,
dust to dust.

Junction

Wait, the next step is so close,
Though in the midst grief all paths seem to have stopped.
Mired brush, sticky footing seems to hold
And confuse in twisted vines of lies,
Drawing blood, tearing, scarring to the core
As darkness seems to fold into slide
As long and slow and slick as blackstrap molasses.
Time seems to ebb in clouded mind.
Days drag in arms reaching, grasping flight,
Yet held, not by mire but by patient love
Permeating this cold, closed junction
To gently extricate toward a new direction,
Unseen, unknown, unwanted in grieving reflection.
How can one move in such a state of shattered dreams,
Knowing this place not as a place of rest,
When the opening for God's greater glory will be sudden?

Baptism

First I had to die—
to myself anyway.
What I controlled,
controlled me—
this was a work of flesh whose works
profited nothing.
Salvation is free—I had only to ask.
First let go
of the world
and become connected
to the energy of the universe—
receive breath, wind, fire,
cleansing through Holy Spirit.
Yet the Spirit was there ever since
I asked the first time, many years ago,
waiting
as I must wait now,
rocking lullaby in God's rest.
Joyous peace is this wait,
five minutes, five years,
until suddenly occurs the miracle
by trust.
Creator God, keep me still but expectant
until You lead me to move.

Death Watch

Spinning is infrequent yet hoped for these days.
Creation always on my mind
during times of stillness that are few
and far between, yet hoped for as a step outside
the box of obligation, this after that,
making it through another day,
Nick's wonderful concerts,
getting twins to bed, dishes put away,
a kiss from Kenny,
breathing,
maybe breathing—something else I like to do.

Then the phone rings.
Someone's actively dying, again,
but it's Ann this time,
only fifty-one,
then Carol, sixty-six, getting younger as I age
and grieve and grieve again.
I'm not even related to but am attached to them,
care so much for each one—
hitting closer to home this time with Ann,
only fifty-one, and with her death
a part of my foundation also dying.
She was always there for the last twenty years;
this has caused such heartache and sadness
and loss for so many.

Yet it puts everything into perspective.

Greater love has no human than to sing
in passionate praise of God—all that matters—
beautiful sounds meshing and vibrating
toward heart song,
spinning differently and drawing breath
as one voice,
easing heart and soul in flowing cry.

My hands long for spinning
to ease the cry,
to create long flowing yarn
from roving carded, brushed, and washed clean,
softly resting in my hands to draw uneven designs
into spindle blurring with speed, becoming strong and constant, yet
changing as the treadle slows. Wool becomes thin.
I change my mind about color.
And it's natural, not paperwork, obligation,
making it through each day—
and it won't die except perhaps to be forgotten
through moving on through another day
doing what I must, longing for the active stillness of spinning ...
Fifty-one years old, sixty-six—
does it really matter
that the house isn't clean
if I've lifted my heart with joy in Godsong
and hugged my family?

Restless Spirit

Soul of Van Gogh
cried out.
Knowing voice screamed soundlessly
inside fleshy walls.
Awaiting escape was painful
to this restless spirit,
brush to canvas its only human interpretation.
Bright landscapes, brilliant hues,
self-portraits
beaten onto canvas after canvas,
still perplexing those who experience their beauty.
Brushes pounced and swirled,
palette knife stroked to perfection
vivid images of light and warmth,
of pain.
Fingertips clutching a tool
painted brilliant clarity of impatient soul,
though mind, knowing spirit too well,
caused self-destruction,
forsook an ear.
Body thrust
into self-inflicted menaces, starvation,
and the pain grew deafening.
Yet rejoice when crows fly,
for spirit at last became free!

This Fallow Time

It seemed the fallow time was during study
While I waited for completion of my tasks,
But see that time was active in the sowing
Of a God seed planted firmly in my past.
The call was urgent though not fully formed,
Necessitating movement immediately.
Direction presented itself through an open door
That led to solid goals before my eyes.
I traveled monthly in a therapeutic dream
Made manifest in healing of my soul
By closing gestalts through tears and revelation,
Polishing skills and gifts to edify and implore.
Formal study done, I feel curled like bud
To bloom and spread in pollinating fashion.
As yet I am held fast by gentle arms,
Yet not idle in longing for extrication.

Grieving

Years are entered and pass in different stages
Of grieving, their sorrows bred by love
Experienced, broken, diseased, deceased, waiting
For other times, anticipating changes
That accompany the embracing process
Of natural emotion, spent and protected by walls
Of memory built stone by stone, erected
Monuments of laughter, tears, joy, and loss.
Places, seasons, remembrances, photos are stored
In quiet chambers of the soul to tremble
Unexpectedly in waves of sensitive pressure,
Heart's pain, mind's numbness, weakened hands taking
Hold of something solid, unmoving, to bear
The weight of sorrow's burden, unbalanced
Sway of losses' loneliness through spirit's sight,
To release in Christ the mired fortress of emotion.

Paradox

Unstable as water, you shall not excel (Genesis 49:4),
Yet vessels influenced can be many and diversely
Guided by flowing bodies toward courses
Fashioned by the Master's hand, not human ingenuity.
Capricious gentles with tenderness dwelling in heart
Exist to minister to hungry of spirit,
Long to touch wounded beings seeking consonance
Through powerful virtue of the unseen Sovereign.
As ebb rises and falls in its cycle,
Waves lift and crash wherever they may.
Solid souls search for waited ways
To love the subtle distraction of mind.
Who's to say but that these mercurial beings
Sail along waves bred by a turn
Of face toward the star brightest now,
Beckoning to be steered into oncoming wind?

Faith

Okay, God, I'm down.
What do You want of me?
I hear "excellence," but how,
when around me status quo is what prevails?
I'm a visionary, but nobody else seems
to be on the same page—
have I totally missed You?
Help me, Creator, to learn Your way,
help me to follow Your steps patiently,
to learn of the process of B to Y,
not just look from A to Z.
My Lord, where must I remain silent?
Where should I speak out and stand firm?
What if there is no energy—can this
common place of status quo
be turned around?
Please, God, help me to listen and
to pray.
I'm praying now, but I fear the pause of dialogue
only to hear silence. You seem to speak
when I'm in the middle of something,
not when I pray—am I doing it wrong?
Please, Holy One, help me not to worry.
I'd like more years of quality life,
to make it past the age of mothering little ones,
do something I want to do, though that seems
so selfish because that's what I strive for now,

wanting to live beyond the constraints
and stresses of growing Your children.
Please forgive me, Lord, for my selfishness
and self-comfort,
for which consequences I fear.
Please, Greatest, forgive the fear
and help me to forgive myself—
I'm doing my best, but not really
if it's not excellent in Your eyes.
I want to be Your servant, Lord, first and foremost.
Please help me!

Here I am in grief, in sadness, lonely
for what, I don't know—
to be taken care of, I guess.
Then before my eyes and my heart
as I mourn again the passing of an age,
an answer appears to remind me
of what I already know,
remind me through the celebration
of a century life of courage, strength, and grace
that how I feel rests not in life's experiences
yet in my response to them—
how simple, how profound,
how difficult to master when in the midst
of winter blues, no matter the season.
Dear Holy Spirit, help me to feel Your truth,
to be patient and wait on You,
to be confident of what I already know,
to be sure for what I hope
and certain of what I do not see.

Inspired by Hebrews 11:1

PART VI

New Life

Afterlife

A concept of reality
is all provided us
in this life.
Only glimpses of clarity
tempt us to voyage
toward afterlife.
For when soul leaves body,
perfect clarity is achieved.
No more looking through the membranes
of a shell.

Lenten Seed

Seeds of paradise—what a concept
when imagining what paradise can be.
Strength of jewels, shine of gold—
magnificent rustle of perfected tree
beyond imagination to consider
just a seed to be glorious
in radiant brilliance,
blinding all who look
upon it then to see
that there is good news to blossom forth
beyond the pale of thought,
humility's gentle breath streaming forth
through God's creation,
not because of, yet within, me.

Way

Look to Me, oh My people.
Look!
How so, Creator God?
It is easier to look about
and to grasp what is seen.
To hold in the hand fruit
of living, reaching arms
that shade heat of day and shatter
brittle limbs in deadly frost.

I Am what beauty rests in better arms,
remaining constant in generous reach,
open sway of will and breath
in meeting small arms reaching
with intention
to touch My transfigured embrace!

Yet your eyes stray aside
to things that sparkle, an invitation
to a different way of will and form
and voice(s) pleasing to ears filled
by white noise, which longs for color,
lush contrast, complex simplicity—
gathered, yet facing outward,
striving for falsehood's grasp, longing
for intangible wealth of store
filling barns—to what gain?

Look to Me, oh My people.
Look!
This expanse of grace
expands eternally, expectant
toward embrace of enigmatic fulcrum—
life, language intelligible to spirit,
soaring *right here* through love!

"Far better to take refuge in God than trust in people"
(Psalm 118:8a MSG) Center Verse in the Bible.

Community Worship

Step outside onto cool grass,
even within dense heat,
as birds sing their brilliant, intermingled calls,
trees stand tall in sway of holy breeze
deeply rooted in tradition and custom.
Reach in new and familiar directions
toward solidarity in Christ—
hospitality as caring stewards of the Gospel
that is life and abundant grace in living.

Leave walls that close us into separate factions
to intermingle as the birds. Raise our voices
to God in song, worship, prayer, and praise—
one people, one voice, a sweet aroma.
Holy Spirit permeates soul as hands raise freely,
reaching upward, outward toward wisdom,
in compassion, through extravagant hospitality.

We are nomads journeying through myriad spheres,
spiritual deserts, and lush forests, reaching
toward extravagant pools of Spirit's presence
to quench our thirst
within community, through living water—
no longer homeless in empty pews, but rich
in moving trust, seeking to be known

and to know by faith
who and whose we are.

Let us rejoice together, through God's Word,
in hymn and dance,
basking together in Sophia hum.

Indwelling

What good is a covenant of grace
when consistently broken
by those to whom grace
is given?
Over and over throughout scripture,
one example after another, grace
is pushed aside for worldly gain.
Pushed—
backward, out of the way
of truth—the love that is always moving
ahead of us right now,
from one height to another,
moving forward with timeless impression
to lead and guide away from self,
toward selfless, community built
in unity of all,
black, brown, yellow, red, white,
united and uniting,
loving close whomever our hearts may choose.
Color, texture, fragrance, growth array
this garden.
Purity swelling wholeness
in diversity, an open playground
of sharing with buzzing and song,
breath of trees, gentle breeze
swaying in glorious whispers.
God persists in frustrated mist

of confused understandings, looking
back to another time
when fertile ground was prepared,
only to be scorched once again
in wiles of disunity and fear.
Another covenant, God meets us
where we are, always moving ahead as well—
not looking back—nor should we.
Always a choice—to allow
or not
pain of change to uplift
like eagles' wings,
fly higher toward one spirit
of love moving back and forth,
indwelling
this temple, you, me,
being emptied into swirls of chaos
to spread love's fragrance over
and over,
having been set free
by shaking off the dust
of oppression!
This is indwelling covenant
of grace, forgiveness and mercy received
and lived into.

Shame Reconciled

Here
there is no time
to be wasted
or lost,
no brokenness
to cause harm.
Light fills, light flows
through, beyond
time,
touching
as gentle caress,
burgeoning sea
in wisps of resplendent
joy.
Here
time is naught,
remembrance ever living
in ecstatic ebullience.
No regret
as wholeness is embraced
in penetrating song.

PART VII

Never the End

Breaking Dishes

Some of the originals
are still perfectly formed
and used with relish--no chips
or cracks.
They are stored among others
whose weakness belies their construction.
And although chips and cracks serve
metaphorically as bearers of use--
perhaps life and energy born as carriers
of nourishment, then cleansed of detritus
for multiple use--they stand,
two set of them--
to me this year--
as poverty's glare.
This grace had been appreciated greatly
when need and hope prevailed
in self-esteem's wither.
Ache of unworthiness set upon shoulders
slumping under its weight.

But now, very slowly, color appears,
a collection of solid
and sturdy pieces of use
without chips and cracks in their future,
to add to perfectly-formed originals
brightening even *closed* cabinets,

meals more often shared now
around family table.

What to do with chipped, cracked dishes?
Should I share this "grace"
to "grace" another family
with *my* glare of brokenness to begin with,
before adding their own?

A shift in spirit beckons,
becomes breath of wholeness awakened
both by this vision
growing as does collection
of color in dish form stacked proudly
one on top of another, slowly growing
as time, self worth, finance, intent allow.
Bits of wholeness grow brighter
as colorful, well-made dishes stack,
and others, weakened, gather below
upon countertop awaiting
intention's brilliant joy
in violent shattering
of once chipped, poorly-constructed dishes--
big bang perhaps,
a scattering shattering through gales
of laughter released
as metaphorical weight lightens,
shoulders raise strong and sturdy,
new light blossoms into a *fiesta!*,
chips, cracks break open, flecks fly everywhere!
Then there is a settling in newly-formed heap
observed with guilt-free curiosity,
swept into dustpan, and emptied
into dark vessel of disposal.

Author Bio

Kristin Aardema Faigh has been writing poetry since age fourteen. She grew up loving the many retold African and Mexican folktales of her grandmother, and author, Verna Aardema. Kristin also grew in her muse through listening to joyful hymns and incredible poetry written, and often published, by her maternal grandmother, Lola E. Hahn, of Florida couplet fame, who wrote *Lolalines*, which Kristin illustrated. Kristin Aardema Faigh is an ordained minister serving in the United Church of Christ. She lives at home in Missouri with her husband, Kenny; her youngest children, twins Austin and Donovan; and her current pet menagerie. Her poem "How Was School Today?" was published in the "Poet to Poet" section of the March 1992 issue of the *Writer* magazine.

Printed in the United States
By Bookmasters